SHIPYARD MUDDLING
AND
MORE MUDDLING
BY RIPYARD CUDDLING

$\left(\begin{array}{c} \text{The Poems of Tyneside} \\ \text{Shipyard Worker Jack Davitt} \end{array} \right)$

EDITED BY KEITH ARMSTRONG

Edited by Keith Armstrong

Photographs by Tony Whittle

Drawings by: Crawford Crowquill
Peter Burns

ISBN 0 906529 13 1

Published by North Tyneside Libraries,
Northumberland Square, North Shields, Tyne & Wear
in association with Northern Voices

Printed by C.V.N. Print, South Shields 091 455 3703

© Jack Davitt 1993

Northern Voices is a member of the Federation of Worker Writers
and Community Publishers

FOREWORD BY TONY BENN

I first read one of Jack Davitt's poems nearly twenty years ago when, as Secretary of State for Industry, I brought Swan Hunter into public ownership and visited the workers in the Yard.

The poem was clear, direct and very perceptive, because it came straight out of his own immense and life-long knowledge of the men who worked in the industry.

It was also very funny indeed, and from that day on I became one of his greatest admirers.

Very few working people ever get their poetry into print and I am delighted that the brilliant poems of Ripyard Cuddling are now to be made available for a wider audience.

He is an exceptionally talented man of whom the North East should be intensely proud, and I hope that this book reaches readers all over the country, because I know that everyone who gets hold of it will enjoy it.

                                            Tony Benn
                                    House of Commons

INTRODUCTION

Poets have often been portrayed as unworldly creatures striking superior postures; a view which has alienated people from their language and denied them the confidence of expressing their own ideas in poetic form. Poetry has been seen as the exclusive preserve of a handful of geniuses, something to be studied rather than written; equally, many poets have not written with an understanding of the real issues which confront the majority of 'ordinary' people. This has, in my view, prevented much of English poetry from communicating to any group of people other than a narrow academic elite. It has become obscure, irrelevant, and turned-in on itself, so much so that its form has often taken precedence over its meaning.

For all of the above reasons, I believe that this definitive collection of poems by Jack Davitt, a former shipyard worker, represents a step in the right direction; a step towards changing the old concepts of elitism which have torn poetry away from positive communication. These poems demonstrate that poetry is a collective craft, a two-way communication between a writer steeped in the experience of his community and an audience which recognises the directness and credibility of his writing. This collection proves too that poetry is a tool for us all - something that is not wielded only by a narrow, chosen, few but is available to everyone. What these poems lack in literary technique they more than make up for in their refreshing openness and accessibility. We need to drag poetry out of the shadows and into the light, and I am sure that this new book will play a humble part in this.

> Keith Armstrong,
> Northern Voices.

SHIPYARD MUDDLING

by
RIPYARD CUDDLING

with drawings by
crawford crowquill

THE END OF THE GAME

My name is Ripyard Cuddling
And writing is my game;
I write of shipyard muddling;
I've won some mild acclaim.

I work for Swan and Hunter,
A welder second grade;
I've never shone at welding
'Cause writing is my trade.

I've worked in Docks and Shipyards
On both sides of the Tyne;
I've toiled on super tankers
And the dreaded "Panel Line".

Ships' managers and foremen
Have fell beneath my pen;
Sir John and Tom McIver
Have felt it now and then.

But everything is changing
And time is running out,
The hanging sword of Damocles
Will fall I have no doubt.

For the berths are lying empty;
The orders running down,
And the time is fast approaching
When Swan Hunter 'Go to town'.

When the drag chains have been fitted
And they launch the final boat,
There'll be scores of jobless welders
And one redundant poet.

THE MEDITATIONS OF AN UNLUCKY WELDER

The water that drips through a hole in the deck
And beats a tattoo on the back of my neck,
And lights that are somehow in just the wrong place;
The burns and the bruises that cover my face;
The juice that is always too fast or too slow;
The staging that's always too high or too low;
The X-Rays on shell butts that must be exact;
The extractor fan pipe that will not extract;
The Foremen who pester with torches and chalk;
Shop Stewards who watch every move like a hawk;
Those sly Sunday workers, the winks and the nods;
That obstructed job with low hydrogen rods;
The buzzer that blows at the start of each day;
The rows with the Foreman to claim C.S.A.;
The tackers with sixes who haven't a clue;
The men with white hats who have nothing to do;
The jobs that can sometimes reduce me to tears;
The caulkers who shatter the drums of my ears;
The halves and the quarters I lose at the gate;
The dark holes and corners where I have my bait;
The box with my gear in that's under the boat;
The nail in the keel block where I hang my coat;
I would swop all these things at the drop of a hat
For a win on the Pools and a chance to grow fat.

WELDER

Welder on your staging plank
High up in the centre tank,
What I wonder are you thinking
Thoughts of horses, women, drinking?

Like a statue standing there,
Haloed by the welding glare,
Now in brightness, now in dark,
Underneath your flashing arc.

Strong of wrist and weak of eye,
Ever reaching for the sky,
Must you realise too late
Overtime's a vicious bait?

Welder in your confined space,
Respirator on your face,
Trusting your extractor fan;
Poor deluded little man.

Like a scarecrow tied together,
Clad in rags and wrapped in leather;
Life for you no bed of roses,
Courting pneumoconiosis.

And there's a lesson you must learn -
There's more to life than what you earn;
You're under unemployment's sword;
You're just a pawn upon the board.

Welder, you're not very wise,
But one day you will realise
That all the things I've said are true -
Until that day, I'll pray for you.

THE TRUTH ABOOT THE WAALL

It was built for the Romans, way back in the past;
They built it with stone, and they built it to last.
Quite a change for the locals from digging for coal
And it kept a large number of men off the dole.

It was the Emperor Hadrian who started it all
When he ordered the peasants to build him this waall.
Just what it was for there was neebody sure
And the reasons he gave were a little obscure.

"This waall," said the Emperor, rubbing his chin,
"Is to stop aall the Picts and the Scots getting in;
Aa'm used to the Geordies, Aa knaa aall their tricks,
But Aa just cannit stomach the Scots and the Picts".

They started the Waall on the banks of the Tyne
And they tried very hard for to keep a strite line.
There were thoosands of Geordies with shovels and picks
And the rate for the job was eleven and six.

The stones for the Waall came by bogie and barrow;
They were cut from the quarries at Hebburn and Jarrow.
They floated them ower the Tyne on a raft,
(Them owld fashioned Geordies could certainly graft).

They travelled to Byker with nivver a spell
But they stopped for a pint when they reached the
                                            "Bluebell".
Then on across meadow and valley and dyke
With nivvor a murmur of trouble or strike.

Onwards they went, heading West all the time,
Still trying their best for to keep a strite line.
In summer they struggled through bracken and heather
And they plodged in the clarts during inclement weather.

They laid the last stone on the second of June
And Hadrian said, "Lads, Aa'm ower the moon,
Aa would like you to knaa that Aa'm proud of you aall,
And Aa thank you aall kindly for building me waall".

A big celebration was held at Carlisle;
They had a grand neet and they done it in style.
The picks and the shovels were aall put away
And the workers were given an extra week's pay.

The Picts and the Scots were a little bit vexed
And voices were raised and muscles were flexed.
But their yelling and shootin' did nee good at aall;
It takes more than taalkin' to get past a waall.

And that is the story, believe it or not,
Of how they defeated the Pict and the Scot;
How the Waall was constructed for one man's enjoyment
And the North East was rescued from mass unemployment.

TANKER ON ICE

Have you worked upon a Tanker in the Winter?
If you have you wouldn't rush to try it twice;
Have you ever crossed a tank to reach a stringer
When the staging planks are thick with snow and ice?

When the sweat begins to freeze inside your collar
Till it forms an icy band around your neck;
When your hand's too numb to grip a metal ladder
And your boot heels have been frozen to the deck.

You will look in vain to find a friendly fire
Or a spot where you can keep your shoulders dry
For there's precious little shelter on a Tanker
When the centre tanks are open to the sky.

Yes it's cruel on a Tanker in the Winter
But a man must do his best to earn a wage;
He's an actor in a Shipyard melodrama
And a Tanker in the Winter is his stage.

When the buzzer breaks the silence of the morning
And a thousand boots are marching down the bank;
With heavy Winter fog around them swirling,
Think of those whose destination is a tank.

But there's nothing much that one can do about it,
Just accept whatever Winter cares to bring;
Every passing day brings April so much nearer
And it's better on a Tanker in the Spring.

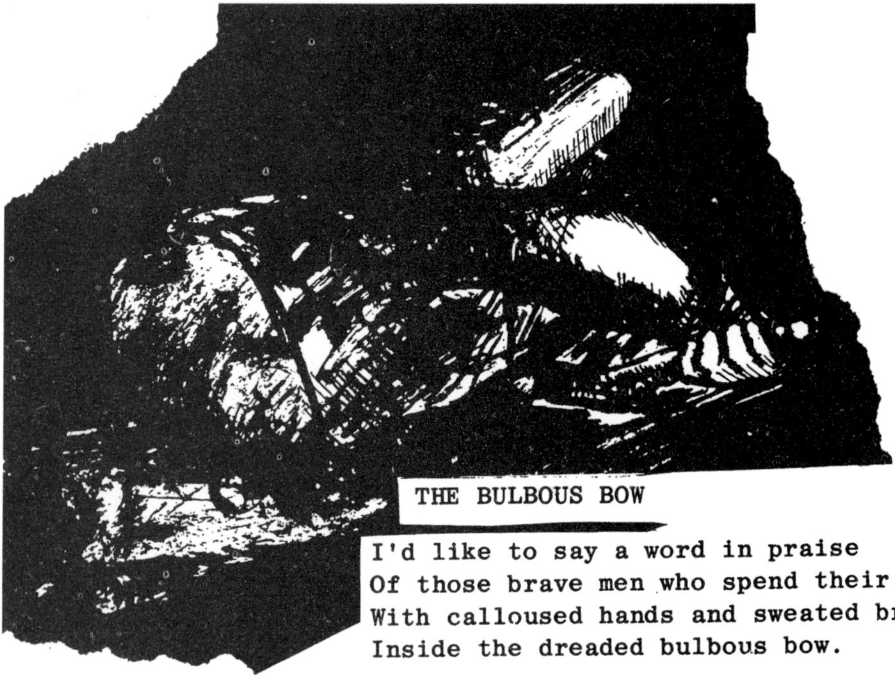

THE BULBOUS BOW

I'd like to say a word in praise
Of those brave men who spend their da
With calloused hands and sweated brow
Inside the dreaded bulbous bow.

I humbly wield my trusty pen
In tribute to these gallant men
And proudly name them here and now
The heroes of the bulbous bow.

How often has a bitter tear
Fell softly in that hemisphere
Where every man's a human mole,
A goldfish in a metal bowl.

And fitter man than you or I,
Who know no roof except the sky,
Who fell the tree or guide the plough
Would perish in the bulbous bow.

yet, within that iron hive,
worker bees of Swan's survive
each of them could tell you how
came to curse the bulbous bow.

, like some malicious stoat,
d grip my guardian angel's throat,
make him promise he'd somehow
erve me from the bulbous bow.

one day I may join the men,
score with "Any eight from ten"
seek fresh fields where I may drowse
to Hell with all your bulbous bows.

LEADERS OF MEN

If managers were blades of grass
And foremen grains of sand,
One half of Swan's would be a field
The other desert land.

If tears could grant me heaven's gifts
Then I'd have some to spare;
If sweat cost thirty bob an ounce,
I'd be a millionaire.

But sweat, alas, is not the thing
To make your fortune grow;
The ones who reap the biggest crops
Are those who do not sow.

If wealth was measured out to each
According to his uses,
Then some in hats of green and white
Would need some good excuses.

There's some of them, aloof and cold,
Who somehow can't be reached,
Like Nixon they daren't say too much
In case they are impeached.

Relations in the industry
Are not too good at all;
There's far too many referees
And too few on the ball.

And so I struggle through it all,
Still faithful to my Class ,
But sometimes how I wish that I
Could be a blade of grass.

DOWNING STREET

The problems for the mangement
Grew bigger every day;
Their numbers were increasing
But no place for them to stay.

So they built a row of offices,
Just like a block of flats,
Where the managers could read their books
and hang their coats and hats.

And there they sit in luxury
And soak each comfort in,
While, down below, the peasants stand
Around their fire tin.

I often marvel at this mass
Of concentrated brain
And wonder how the floor supports
Could ever take the strain.

This row of flats, this "Downing Street",
This intellectual den,
Oh how I wish I had the brain
To join these clever men.

But peasants mustn't venture near
In case they cause infection,
Just bend the knee, or bow the head,
In "Downing Street's" direction.

I bear no grudge, nor envy feel,
Just slightly sick and chocker;
'Cause I've been trying eighteen months
To get a flaming LOCKER.

GEORDIE'S BONANZA

Just off the coast at Seaton Sluice
A drilling rig struck orange juice
And all the locals clapped their hands
And queued with bottles on the sand.

An expert from the USA
Took samples of the juice away
And after scrutiny and test
Declared it was the very best.

From miles around reporters came,
The North East coast was tasting fame,
They said ten million barrels lay
Between the "Sluice" and Whitley Bay.

A group of local leading lights,
Well versed in verbal brawls and fights,
Decided that the time had come
To pluck this unexpected plum.

They reasoned that, with Geordie backing,
Support for them would not be lacking;
They'd keep the juice and then demand
Home rule at once for Geordieland.

But, though their banner fluttered proud
And Geordie voices clamoured loud,
The government was not amused
And Geordie claims were all refused.

A million Geordies homeward trailed,
Their spirits low, their mission failed,
No traces of their former glee;
Home rule alas was not to be.

Defeated in their final fight,
And just when things had looked so bright
Their show of strength had been no use;
They had to share the orange juice.

But Geordie don't abandon hope;
You mustn't sit around and mope,
For better things may come to pass;
They're drilling now for North Sea Bass.

A WELDER'S NURSERY RHYME

Tinker, Tailor, Soldier, Sailor,
Have you heard from Walter Taylor?
Is your name upon the List?
Have you hit or have you missed?

Mirror, Mirror on the wall,
Where will Walter's chopper fall?
Some may get a big surprise
When he cuts them down to size.

Eeny, Meeny, Miny, Mo,
Who will stay and who will go?
Who will get the Pay-off Notes?
I wonder if he's sacking Poets?

Twinkle, Twinkle little star
D'you want to buy a Motor Car?
Plenty on the market soon;
With luck we'll buy them back in June.

Little Boy Blue come blow your horn
And see the Welders all forlorn,
Just like a row of ragged Tramps,
Each one with a book of Stamps.

Fee and Fi and Fo and Fum,
We're from Swan's Consortium;
Here comes McIver to close down the Shed
And here comes the chopper to chop
                      off your head.

THE PRESENTATION

After twenty five years they gave Geordie a watch;
Twenty five years in the same dreary notch.
They allowed him ten minutes to wash and to shine,
For to straighten his cap and to get into line.

He stood in a row with another sixteen,
And they posed for a snap for the Work's magazine.
A company director presented the watch;
He shook Geordie's hand and he filled him a Scotch.

This important occasion had George in a flap
And he didn't quite know what to do with his cap.
He was out of his depth with these folk from the top
And he wished he was back at his bench in the shop.

Fine speeches were made by the cream of the firm
And the bouquets they handed made poor Geordie squirm.
There was one of the speakers, a man of great girth,
Who described men like George as "The salt of the earth"

There was patting of backs and they sang "Auld Lang Syne"
There was plenty to eat and a surplus of wine.
They were toasted in whisky and showered with praise
And George and his pals spent the night in a daze.

But Geordie was glad when they called it a day
And when him and his mates had at last slipped away.
He loosened his tie, rubbed the sweat off his head,
Then he felt more himself, and his face was less red.

Then he looked at the watch which was clutched in his hand;
It was still in its box and it really looked grand.
He had bought it with sweat, but the price wasn't dear
For the cost to the firm had been ten bob a year.

FLAT OUT

Two Half Shifts and a Sunday Lad,
A Saturday as well;
The Bans have all been lifted Lad;
We'll have a peaceful spell.

And never mind the sequence Lad,
Weld everything you see;
Pull out all the stops Lad;
There'll be bags of L.S.D.

The Launch must be on time Lad,
You can beat the Jap;
Help production climb Lad;
You're no Andy Capp.

Lap up all the cream Lad,
And watch that undercut;
Five men to a seam Lad;
Four men to a Butt.

But when this Great Day comes Lad,
Our ship has gone to Sea,
It's Prudhoe Street for you Lad,
And West Moor Dole for me.

SHIPYARD PATTER

DEPRESSION

I stood in Wallsend shipyard
And looked across the Tyne
The river of my homeland
More famous than the Rhine.

The yard of Hawthorn Leslies
Lay spread before my gaze
The birthplace of the 'Kelly'
In those distant wartime days.

The berths were still and empty
The cranes stood stark and still
I admit my heart was heavy
And my eyes began to fill.

Like a vision from the 'Thirties'
I can't forget that scene
The grass was taking over
The berths were turning green.

Yes they're growing grass at Leslies
Where once they built the best
And they're closing down the Fab Shed
The yard's been laid to rest.

And further up the river
Where the K.G.5 was built
The weeds have claimed the gantries
And the ways are clogged with silt.

The days of work and plenty
Are well and truly gone
And the famous Tyneside shipyards
Are closing one by one.

And what about the future?
What will tomorrow bring?
When the men of Swan and Hunter
Face unemployment's sting?

What will become of Walker
When inertia grips the Tyne
Will Wallsend be a ghost town
Will Hebburn face decline?

But maybe this disaster
Is a blessing in disguise
From the embers of the shipyards
A 'Phoenix' may arise.

And the Geordie of tomorrow
Will hold his head up high
When the cranes have been demolished
And his bairns can see the sky.

There'll be no more double bottoms
Opportunities galore
In a land that's fit for heroes
(Have I heard those words before?)

We'll be happy and contented
In that 'Eden' by the Tyne
All our cares will be forgotten
And the sun will always shine................

These thoughts and many others
Went racing through my head
As I gazed across the river
At the shipyard that was dead.

I sadly stood there dreaming
As poets sometimes do
And I prayed some glorious morning
My dreams will all come true.

DICKIE'S OVERTIME

Dickie loved his overtime
He'd work around the clock
And when they asked for volunteers
He always led the flock.

Just like a donkey engine
He never took a spell
He'd work right through his Xmas break
And Boxing Day as well.

No matter what the weather sent
Through rain or hail or snow
You'd see him working up aloft
Or toiling down below.

And all the foremen loved him
He played the game their way
If any job should fall behind
"Old Dick" would always stay.

No matter what the day was
They only had to ask
And like a shot "Wor Dick" was there
Complete with bait and flask.

His bank account grew fatter
He bought a brand new car
And everybody prophesised
That Dick would travel far.

Now Dick was always healthy
His cheeks were pink and shiny
But though his heart was big and strong
His brain was rather tiny.

For health, my friend, is not a crop
There's no way you can reap it
And working round the clock, alas
Is not the way to keep it.

His step began to falter
His cheeks grew drawn and pale
His eye no longer sparkled
And his health began to fail.

A sad and ghostly shadow
Was all that remained of Dick
The overtime had took its toll
Now Dick was on the sick.

For seven years he lay around
A sad and sorry figure
And as his bank book dwindled
His weekly debts grew bigger.

At last poor Dick surrendered
And drew his final breath
The overtime he loved so much
Had caused poor Dickie's death.

He was laid to rest at Benton
Where the apple blossoms drift
His workmates missed the funeral
They were working half a shift.

This story is a sad one
And yet my friend it's true
So please beware of overtime
For Dickie could be YOU.

THE MAURETANIA

Number one berth, Swan and Hunter
That is where My story starts
When the good ship Mauretania
Won a million Geordie hearts.

She was big and she was bonnie
She was leader of the line
She was Queen of the Atlantic
And her birth place was the Tyne.

She was high and wide and handsome
And she nearly touched the sky
When they launched her that September
Not one Geordie eye was dry.

She was built with skill and patience
And with Geordie love and care
Only Geordies could have built her
Only Geordies have that flair.

It was on her maiden voyage
That the "Maurie" shook the world
When she smashed the crossing record
With the British flag unfurled.

The coveted Blue Riband
The "Maurie" took with ease
And she reigned for more than twenty years
The Monarch of the seas.

And wherever Geordies gather
You will hear them talk with pride
Of the good ship Mauretania
The toast of all Tyneside.

Of one thing I am certain
As I put away my pen
The world will never ever see
The like of her again.

SWAN HUNTER'S ROBOT

When piecework was abolished
And welders went on time
Production in the Fab Shed
Began a downward climb.

So the management decided
That something must be done
To boost production up again
New orders must be won.

One very senior manager
Unto his colleagues said
"I think I have the answer
To the problems in the shed.

We'll copy British Leyland
And have our sheds re-kitted
If we can't make our welders work
We'll have a robot fitted".

The management applauded
This very clever scheme
For managers are not as daft
As they sometimes seem.

One sunny Monday morning
Just as I drew my card
I saw a very strange machine
Come marching through the yard.

It didn't have a driver
It travelled unattended
It was a robot, nothing less
The welders' reign was ended.

A group of smiling managers
Put the robot through it s test
And judging by remarks I heard
They were very much impressed.

It tackled and welded brackets
Completed seams and butts
Each job was scaled and polished
No scars or undercuts.

The gaffers were delighted
Their faces wreathed in smiles
For every foot a welder done
The robot done three miles.

The management decided
There would have to be a place
For the robot on the night shift
It must work for Geordie Pace.

"The best laid plans of mice and men"
The Scottish poet said
"Don't always work the way you want--"
This happened in the shed.

The nightshift were astounded
When the robot came in view
And the night's work was completed
By twenty five to two.

Now the robot wasn't programmed
To be destitute of work
When they tried to turn the juice off
That is when it went berserk.

With flashing eyes and waving arms
It lurched across the yard
Advancing on the gatehouse
It terrified the guard.

Then it headed for the High street
As the guard informed his mate
But before it left the shipyard
It put three runs round the gate.

Up Station Road it thundered
Like a super sonic jet
It destroyed the Wallsend Forum
And it wrecked the "Penny Wet".

Around the Metro Station
It scampered hell for leather
It grabbed two yellow buses
And welded them together.

Two hundred local coppers
and a squad from S.A.S.
Were assisted by the Army
To help sort out the mess.

But the robot wasn't finished
There was still more work to do
Two runs around the "Duke of York"
Then down the Avenue.

Swan's Dock was overwhelmed
The robot had a ball
It left two tankers shattered
Behind the dockyard wall.

Policemen helped the injured
And informed the next of kin
But the robot's run was ending
The net was closing in.

As the sun arose that morning
Just like a giant cherry
The robot left the stricken Dock
And headed for the ferry.

Now its sights were set on Jarrow
That town of song and wine
But it stumbled on the landing stage
And plunged into the Tyne.

The Swan and Hunter robot
Was never seen again
Off the ferry stage that morning
It took the count of ten.

Then Swans got back to normal
They tidied up the town
the "Penny Wet" re-opened
And they swept the High Street down.

The memory of that robot
And the night it ran amok
Will forever be remembered
By the shipyard and the dock.

And Geordie Pace's nightshift
I'm led to understand
Do not require robots
They'll weld each job by hand.

CHECKMATE

What's happened to the shipyards
Where I used to earn my bread?
They've clobbered Hawthorn Leslies
And the Naval Yard is dead.

The berths are standing empty
The cranes have turned to rust
The Platers' sheds have crumbled
And surrendered to the dust.

The Wallsend and the Neptune Yards
Are standing on the brink
As they stutter on one cylinder
Must these two giants sink?

For economic reasons
Our ancient crafts must rot
And money must be saved they say
For who? for why? for what?

And Britain will be poorer
When Tyneside closes down
And the curse of unemployment
Invades old Wallsend Town.

And meanwhile what of Hebburn
Where work was once abundant?
And Walker too, when active men
Are written off redundant?

So shed a tear for Tyneside
And for the Shipyard men
And pray that soon each one of them
Will be in work again.

And in the months ahead perhaps
Your prayers will be fulfilled
And this unbending Government
Will sanction 'Scrap and build'.

MORE MUDDLING BY CUDDLING

AUTOBIOGRAPHY

My cap too big, my bait too small,
I stood beside the shipyard wall.
The buzzer ringing in my ears,
I remember I was close to tears.

My school books had been put away
For this was my first working day,
And I was at a tender age,
A question mark on life's first page.

I saw the workmen hurry past
And felt my courage melting fast.
Bewildered in a strange terrain,
I looked for sympathy in vain.

With eager eyes I searched each face,
Each runner in that morning race,
But they had troubles of their own
And I was left to stand alone.

But youth will always have its way
And somehow I survived that day,
And that was how it all began,
That morning I became a man.

Apprenticed to the welding trade,
I struggled hard to make the grade.
The squarest peg, the roundest hole-
The choice was this, or digging coal.

I often think, on looking back,
That somewhere I went off the track.
The road I took was wrong somehow-
I've plenty time to rue it now.

For forty years my cheeks were wet
With shipyard tears and shipyard sweat.
I've hurried to the buzzer's call
And toiled on vessels large and small.

I often wonder, can it be?
That boy so long ago was me?
That boy so innocent and green,
That 'Never was', who might have been.

As I recall those distant years,
And see myself so close to tears;
My cap was not too big at all-
It was my head that was too small.

ELEGY ON A TYNESIDE SHIPYARD

I was born to be a loser
beneath the minus sign,
And was doomed to be a welder
In the shipyards of the Tyne.
I have toiled in "Hawthorn Leslie's"
And I've sweated with the best.
I have struggled hard
In the "Naval Yard"
And in "Swan's" both East and West.

I have had my fill of forepeaks
And I'm sick of engine rooms,
And my eyes have cried for mercy
From the sting of welding fumes.
I recall the days of piecework
When I risked my health for gold
And my only God
Was a welding rod
And the job was never cold.

Those days have gone forever,
They'll never come again,
But they left their mark behind them
On a thousand broken men.
Now the ships are getting bigger,
The tanks are bigger too,
But there's still a place
In a confined space
For the likes of me and you.

When the shipyard gates are opened
And the morning buzzers blow,
And the bank is black with workers
All reluctant for to go,
You can quickly spot a welder,
He's the one that looks like death,
But you mustn't scoff
When you hear him cough
And you see him fight for breath.

There's just one thing keeps me going
As I fight to keep my health,
It's the thought that I might make it
In my quest for worldly wealth.
Just to check my football coupon
And to find a winning line;
That will be my day
But, till then, I'll stay
Beneath the minus sign.

MONDAY MORNING

From my cosy bed in winter
To the early morning street,
To the bus queue on the corner,
Where I curse, and stamp my feet.

Bait-bag slung across my shoulder,
And a Woodbine in my hand,
Daily Mirror in my pocket,
Discontentedly I stand.

Shoulders hunched against the weather,
Collar turned against the rain,
Streaming eyes, and headache pounding,
Monday morning once again.

Was it only nine short hours
Since I sang, and waved my glass?
Half-past ten till half-past seven,
How the sleeping hours pass!

Buses coming, buses going,
Thunder past the waiting queue,
Sleepy faces at the windows;
Room for us, but not for you.

Then, at last, a double-decker
Pulls up, when all hope seems gone.
Silently, each weary figure
Troops aboard her, one by one.

Standing, swaying in the gangway,
Glancing at the Racing Page,
One more smoke, then back among it.
What one does to earn a wage!

Early buzzer splits the morning,
Ghostly figures hurry by,
Muted voices, void of laughter,
To the shipyard gates they fly.

This, then, is my Monday morning.
This, the cross I have to bear.
Every working man an island,
None to help, and none to care.

None to lend a friendly shoulder,
Not one smile to warm my day.
On a cheerless Monday morning,
Laughter rarely comes my way.

So I pray, that, come tomorrow,
Monday's gloom will fade and die,
And my burden will be lighter,
Underneath a Tuesday sky.

Merry nights make sorry mornings,
So the local sages say,
But, as long as there's a Friday,
Monday blues are here to stay.

ONE MAN AND HIS BIKE

Bill Robson was a miner,
One of the rank and file,
And, though he worked unsocial hours,
He always wore a smile.

By bike each day he travelled,
Through hail and sleet and rain
He pedalled six long miles to work
And six miles back again.

Some went by public transport,
And some were known to hike,
But Bill was never seen without
His ever faithful bike.

The bike was rather ancient,
It lacked that modern shine
And some parts could be dated back
To eighteen ninety nine.

The brakes were rusted solid,
The seat was tied with string,
The back wheel had no mudguard
And the bell refused to ring.

Each time Bill pushed the pedal
It groaned, but tried its best,
For what the old bike needed
Was a long and well earned rest.

To work on Sunday fore shift
As up the hills they toiled,
The poor old bike was always dry
But Bill was always oiled.

At sixty five precisely,
Old Bill gave up the pit.
His faithful bike was laid to rest,
The time had come to quit.

But Bill still travels daily
With his 'United' pass.
You'll see him in the 'Allotment Club',
Behind a well-filled glass.

And what about the poor old bike?
How fares his faithful steed?
Well, for your information, friend,
It's done quite well indeed.

In Old Bill Robson's living room,
Above the fireplace,
The grand old bike hangs proudly
In a fancy guilded case.

So both of them are happy,
No need to shed a tear,
The old bike gets the glory,
Bill Robson gets the beer.

A DAY OF REST

Like silent statues made of wood,
A group of nightshift welders stood
That Sunday morn at half past eight,
With anxious eyes upon the gate.

And no one spoke among that crowd
And every nightshift head was bowed;
They stood there silent, fingers crossed,
A member of their team was lost.

At half past seven in the Yard,
Each nightshift man had drawn his card
And everyone was present - bar
Their top performer, Jackie Parr.

And that was why they gathered there
Beside the gate to stand and stare,
But still the bank remained quite clear
And even Wilcox shed a tear.

For Jackie never missed a trick
And whether sober, drunk, or sick,
Come snow or sleet, come rain or hail,
"Wor Jack" was never known to fail.

But fail he did that Sunday morning,
An absentee who gave no warning,
And those who knew him sadly said
"Poor Jackie Parr is surely dead".

The Welders had a "Whip around"
And Norman Collins gave a pound;
MacKenzie gave a half a crown
And Jimmy Jordan gave a frown.

The treasurer was Geordie Pace
And, with a grin upon his face,
He promised he would do his best
To spend it all on Jack's last rest.

At one o'clock the buzzer blew
And homeward went the nightshift crew,
Some by bus and some by car,
And each one prayed for Jackie Parr.

Come Monday night, those nightshift men
Were back in overalls again,
A "quick one" at the "Penny Wet",
Then back among the toil and sweat.

But in the Yard, surprise, surprise,
Before those startled nightshift eyes
Stood Jackie Parr in leather wrap,
Complete with nineteen forty cap.

And, even now, there's none can say
What happened on that Sabbath day
But I, for one, discovered signs
That helped me read between the lines.

Next evening on my way from work
I called in at the "Duke of York"
And, drinking in the Buffet Bar,
Were Geordie Pace and Jackie Parr.

THE CLOSED SHOP

A welder and a caulker stood
Outside the golden gate.
Unto the welder Peter said
"Come in and bring your mate."

"Now tell me lads," the great man said,
When he had got them in,
"What did you do down there below
And are you free from sin?"

"I worked for Swan's" the caulker said,
"And all my life I toiled.
I always kept my sidecut sharp;
My machine was always oiled."

"But as for sins, I must admit,
I sometimes took a flier
But on the job I done my bit;
I always was a trier."

"I struggled with the toughest jobs,
I sweated in the tanks,
And, now my spell on earth is done,
It's time I had some thanks."

"God bless you lad," the great man said,
"I knew of all these things
And here's an order signed by me
For halo, harp, and wings."

Then turning to the welder chap,
He looked into his eyes
"And what did you accomplish lad?
I don't want any lies."

The welder stood and thought awhile
And slowly scratched his head
"I worked for Swan and Hunter too,
For twenty years," he said.

"I was a 'Shoppy' all my life,
A leader of the many;
I wrung from Swan's an honest wage
And fought for every penny."

"I argued for conditions
In coffer dam and tank,
And, when the men weren't satisfied,
I led them up the bank."

"I broke the 'Social contract'
Extracting what I could;
I fought Swan Hunter tooth and nail
Like all good shoppies should."

"I spoke to stike committeees
And made them toe the line,
Encouraging the militants
On both sides of the Tyne."

"And that's my story, Peter,
I hope you'll be approving;
I've got both feet inside your gate;
I hope I won't be moving."

St. Peter took him by the hand
And led him from the gate:
"Just stay there for a while," he said,
"You won't have long to wait."

"You're in the wrong department, lad,
The lines have gotten crossed,
But there's a man will come for you.
Don't worry, you're not lost."

"He'll take you to your Kingdom Come
Beyond yon Heav'nly lawns.
You can't mistake him when he comes,
He wears a pair of horns."

ROGER BUNG

This is the story of Roger Bung
Who sacrificed his starboard lung,
A sample of those silly types
Who work without extractor pipes.

And whether in or out of doors,
Or using iron powder fours,
In coffer dams and engine rooms,
Poor Roger gobbled all the fumes.

Through Summer heat and Winter cold,
He laboured in his quest for gold
But, in his quest for worldly wealth,
This foolish welder wrecked his health.

Before the shrine of overtime,
He knelt and watched his savings climb
But what's the use of gold or treasure
To one with neither lung nor leisure?

Then came the day, as come it must,
When Roger's hopes were turned to dust,
The Doctor shook his head and said
"I sentence you to twelve months' bed."

Away from fumes and C.S.A.,
Poor Roger Bung soon passed away
And welders came from Tyne and Wear
To say goodbye and shed a tear.

At St. Bartholomew's, alas,
He lies beneath the churchyard grass;
At peace in his last resting place,
He's found his final confined space.

Above the grave where Roger lies,
A marble cross points to the skies
And written by an unknown poet,
Upon that cross there words (I quote):

"Please say a prayer for Roger Bung
Who lies here minus starboard lung,
If he had used a fan it's true,
He might have lived to pray for you."

BY GUM

I broke my teeth in Swan's canteen,
They weren't as tough as they might have been;
They coped with the chips and the beans and such,
But the Yorkshire pud was just too much.

And now I sit, forlorn and glum,
And run my tongue along my gum.
I cannot smile, like Edward Heath,
Because, you see, I have no teeth.

There's many more like me who tried
To battle through a plate of fried;
Who finished up in Wallsend Green,
And left their teeth in Swan's canteen.

God bless the canteen staff, who share
The grub around with loving care,
Undaunted by the jeers and boos,
Flung at them by the toothless queues.

If I could start from scratch again,
I'd leave those "Must have dinner men",
And join that older, wiser, group
Who only risk their teeth on soup.

These days I travel for my grub
And, in the "Coronation Club",
You'll find me in the bar, where I,
Will settle for a pint and pie.

THE LEATHER QUEEN

She sits in splendour all alone,
Like Cleopatra on her throne.
And navigates an old machine;
She's Swan and Hunter's "Leather Queen."

She'll stitch your glove or mend your cape,
Or put your apron back in shape;
There is no charge, she sends no bill,
If you need gloves, just ask for Lil.

Her place of work is near the store,
There's heaps of leather on the floor,
And there, amid this busy scene,
Is Lily Groves the "Leather Queen."

There's always plenty work to do,
Repairing old, or making new,
And welders queue outside her door,
From early morn till half past four.

And there, behind her bench, she sits
And patches aprons, gloves, and mitts;
She gives you service with a smile
And leather in the latest style.

And, when you feel that Winter chill,
Do not despair, just go to Lil;
And, if you're working on the boat,
She'll fit you with a leather coat.

And if it ever came to pass
That we should lose our "Leather Lass,"
You'd see production figures fall,
For soon we'd have no gloves at all.

So Swan and Hunter please take note,
And listen to this humble Poet:
If you want progress to be seen
Look after Lil the "Leather Queen."

DESPERANDUM

I sit here on my staging plank
And gaze around this cursed tank.
It's full of fumes, it's badly lit,
And nothing, nowhere, seems to fit.

There's broken handrails everywhere
But no one ever seems to care;
There's crooked ladders out of place,
That only lead to empty space.

Falling sparks and rising smoke;
Welding fumes, that cling and choke;
Blower pipes that will not blow,
And Foreman dashing to and fro.

Pockets where the shadows lie;
Lugs and dogs that sometimes fly;
Scrap that falls without a warning;
Caulkers on a Monday morning.

Panic reigning all the while;
Managers who never smile,
Men in white, and men in green
Dashing round the busy scene.

Three half shifts, and every Sunday;
Splitting headache every Monday.
Will this nightmare never end?
Soon I'll be right round the bend.

Still I sit upon my plank,
And gaze around this cursed tank.
The fumes are quickly growing thicker,
But I am getting sicker, quicker.

Bow under construction at
Wallsend (from Hebburn Hall)
Peter Burns 1978

HERBERT THE MANAGER

Herbert was a manager,
At least that's what they said,
Sometimes he managed on the ship
And sometimes in the shed.

His shoes were black and shiny,
His helmet snowy white,
He strutted round the yard by day
And he swaggered home each night.

And Herbert spoke to no one
When he was on the job,
For Herbert was a manager
And Herbert was a snob.

Just what it was he managed
No one could really tell,
But Herbert bluffed his way along
And he managed very well.

At launching celebrations
And such like posh affairs,
He never got invited
Though he tried his best for years.

When the lady with the flowers
Swung the bottle at the ship,
He would stand beneath the platform
And a tear would start to slip.

The tears would flow quite freely
When the gentry all had gone,
For Herbert's place was with them
Rubbing shoulders with Sir John.

For Herbert was important,
A manager no less,
Though what it was he managed
Was anybody's guess.

The workers too ignored him,
They made him feel quite small,
And sometimes Herbert wondered
Why he managed them at all.

A Company director
Crossed Herbert's path one day
And asked him what his function was
And how he earned his pay.

"If you can't tell," said Herbert
"You really must be slow,
My dear chap, I'm a manager,
I manage things you know."

Now, Company directors
Can sometimes make it hot;
This one did for Herbert,
He sacked him on the spot.

Now Herbert is redundant
He plays a brand new role;
He's learned like us, the hard way,
To 'Manage' on the dole.

This story has two morals:
For power do not quest
And never cross Directors -
You'll come off second best.

THE CORRIDORS OF POWER

What is it that becomes a man
When put in charge of others?
What makes him change his attitude
Towards his former brothers?

Did God in his great wisdom
Upon this man bestow
Some kind of magic quality
He never had before?

Is there a secret fountain
Where knowledge can be gained?
Where normal men go in to drink
And come out fully trained?

And why must every candidate
To this exclusive band
Decide to exercise on me
His powers of command?

How often in the still of night,
When thoughts keep sleep at bay,
I've thought about those clever men;
Why can't I be like they?

Why can't I strut around the deck,
White helmet on my head,
And demonstrate to all that I'm
The leader, not the led?

In coffer dams and engine rooms,
I'd proudly do my stuff;
The Monarch of the shipyard scene
Swan Hunter's Brian Clough.

But these are only empty dreams,
No substance, more's the pity,
I'm not a Brian Clough at all,
I'm just a Walter Mitty.

So let me dream my dreams away
Like Flannigan and Allen.
By day I'm just a half a pint,
By night I am a gallon.

But through these jumbled thoughts of mine
There's still one question bothers......
What is it that becomes a man
When put in charge of others?

THE LEGEND OF THE MILLION TON TANKER

A group of yards along the Tyne
Decided they would all combine
To pool their skills and then, perhaps,
United they would beat the Japs.

The early Spring of 'Sixty Eight'
Saw all these brains behind one gate,
By August their endeavours won
A tanker of a million ton.

This order set the Tyne alight,
The future now at last looked bright,
And so they booked the City Hall
To hold a celebration ball.

The ball was quite a grand affair
And everyone of note was there
And members of the working class
Rubbed shoulders with the upper brass.

A merry night was had by all
At Swans' amalgamation ball
But all good things must end it's true
And there was still a job to do.

Production soon got under way
And the keel was down by Guy Fawkes' Day;
A mighty keel of six inch plate,
It stretched from Swans' to Walkergate.

The longy butts were ten feet high,
They made the strongest caulkers cry
And platers laboured in the sheds
With tie plates big as wing bulkheads.

The stagers all wore parachutes
And rubber suckers on their boots;
One counter name of Bobby Corbett
Fell off the mast - he's still in orbit.

The journey to the after peak
On foot took half a working week.
And, though the workers had to hike,
Each gaffer had a motor bike.

The centre tanks were such a height
The upper deck was out of sight.
And, up among the beams and struts,
Two helicopters checked the butts.

Inside the bulbous bow one day
Two foremen welders lost their way;
Alas! these two intrepid men
Were never ever seen again.

The human mind could scarcely grip
The magnitude of this great ship;
This miracle of Tyneside skill
Was, for the Japs, a bitter pill.

It wasn't just the Japanese
That Swan and Hunter failed to please;
Before the launching celebrations
The town would need some alterations.

The council sat in grim debate
And hammered out the township's fate.
They talked all day of sweat and toil
That night they burned the midnight oil.

Upon the map they drew a mark
From Carville Road to Wallsend Park;
The drag chains for the giant ship
Would run right through this fated strip.

The Mayor arose and sad of voice
Said, "Gentlemen, we have no choice,
Although we love our dear old town,
We'll have to pull half of it down.

The 'Mem' and the Masonic Hall
And Woolworths too will have to fall,
The 'Ship' the 'Penny Wet' as well
And even Simpson's Grand Hotel".

The morning sky the sun was greeting
When Wallsend council left their meeting
And civic heads were bowed with cares,
And civic cheeks were wet with tears.

But hope forever springs eternal
For there in that same morning's 'Journal'
Was news that gladdened every eye,
In the next verse I will tell you why.......

The news on pages one and two
Came like a bolt out of the blue -
The ship built by the great combine
Was two feet wider than the Tyne.

The council all began to sing,
The Mayor danced a highland fling,
And passers-by turned round to stare
At civic duts tossed in the air.

The council's cup of joy was full
But elsewhere hopes were rather dull;
The heads of Swan and Hunter's group
Were well and truly in the soup.

The brains assembled in their lair,
Sir John himself was in the chair -
"The problem gentlemen (I quote)
Is how to get our ship afloat."

They sat all day and made their plans
And ended with a show of hands;
Their scheme, though born of desperation,
Resolved a tricky situation.

On Monday, June the twenty third,
The most amazing launch occurred,
They turned the berth the other way
And launched the ship at Whitley Bay.

It thundered past the 'Rising Sun'
This monster of a million ton,
High Farm Estate and Bigges Main
Will never be the same again.

No architect could ever cure
The damage done to Shiremoor
And all agreed it was a pity
The drag chains wrecked the Spanish City.

The backwash when it hit the sea
Drowned fifty pigs at Peterlee,
The B.B.C. reported panic
When monster crabs invaded Alnwick.

At last the giant super tanker
In sixty fathoms lay at anchor,
A massive structure painted grey
It brooded over Whitley Bay.

Three shifts of fitters toiled like slaves
As this great monster rode the waves,
Completing in one busy year
The engine and the steering gear.

The happy day arrived at last
When, pennants flying from her mast,
The giant ship got under way
And left the shores of Whitley Bay.

But trouble seemed to dog this ship
For, early on her maiden trip,
She turned to starboard off Penzance
And dislocated half of France.

De Gaulle, who seemed a trifle vexed,
To Wilson said "Whatever next?
Your ship has caused grave complications
I'm off to tell United Nations".

A block vote by the 'Iron Curtain'
And the tanker's fate was sealed for certain,
In spite of Harold Wilson's pleas
They banned her from the seven seas.

Mid scenes of grief and deep emotion
They towed her to the Arctic Ocean
And there in that far Northern clime
She's doing penance for her crime.

Though politicians fought her case,
They couldn't save the tanker's face.
In spite of all their flowery words,
She's now a sanctuary for birds.

Out there, beneath the Arctic skies,
A part of France's coast-line lies
And traces too, you can be sure,
Of Bigges Main and Shiremoor.

CREDO

It's written in the Holy Book
That blessed are the poor,
With less possessions on their backs
Their problems will be fewer.

And further down the page, it says
That blessed are the meek
It then goes on to glorify
The virtues of the weak.

Now I don't want to argue
With the writing of the ''Sages''
For who am I to criticise
Those holy, hallowed pages?

But I can't help but think sometimes
Myself both poor and weak,
That the tongue of he who wrote these words
Was firmly in his cheek.

TWO THINGS

There's two things every man must have,
His happiness to measure:
The first is money, need you ask?
The other one is leisure.

But neither goal can be attained
Without some extra bother;
In order to achieve the one,
You sacrifice the other.

And, though we fight on every front
For economic growth,
There's some with neither ease nor wealth,
And some a glut of both.

For fifty years a man may strive
His living to ensure,
And still be, at the end of play,
A member of the poor.

But, meanwhile, on the other hand,
The Boss's son gets stronger;
His salary the years increase,
His holidays grow longer.

For one's an old Etonian
And one's from Council school;
One was meant to bend the knee,
The other born to rule.

If I could gather in the cards
That life has dealt these men,
I'd like to 'cut' them fair and square
And deal them out again.

And, maybe, with a little luck,
Their roles will be reversed,
And, just for once, a working man
Can say "I came in first".